From Job Interview To Job Offer

A Quick Guide to Interviewing Success

From Job Interview To Job Offer

A Quick Guide to Interviewing Success

Obi Okere

From Job Interview to Job Offer
Copyright © 2012 by Obi Okere

Cover by: Uche Okere

All rights reserved. No part of this book may be reproduced in any form by any electronic or mechanical means including photocopying, recording, or information storage and retrieval without permission in writing from the author.

ISBN-13: 978-1480094581

ISBN-10: 1480094587

www.realizeyourpeak.com

Printed in U.S.A.

To my mom and dad, Joy: my girlfriend and best friend, and my brothers and sisters: Ijeoma, Amanze, Kelechi, Chidinma, and Uche. Thank you for your continued support and for always believing in my success.

Table of Contents

Introduction 1
Chapter 1
The Job Seeker's Winning Philosophy 4
Chapter 2
Why Employers Hire Candidates 7
Chapter 3
Creatively Selling Yourself to Employers 11
Chapter 4
Tools to Bring With You to the Interview 19
Chapter 5
The Interview Process 27
Chapter 6
The Psychology of Negotiation 43
Chapter 7
Creating More Interviews With More Employers .. 51
Chapter 8
Staying Motivated Throughout the Process 57

Introduction

If you are a job seeker looking to make the best impression for a current job interview or a future one, this book is for you. Doing well in a job interview is not an easy task, especially when you are competing with other qualified candidates. There is a certain mindset needed to artfully navigate a job interview process and receive the privilege of landing the job: the mindset of a salesman. You represent a company. That company is (your name) Inc. Your product is your personal service. You are the number one salesperson of that service. No one can sell it better than you.

Great salespeople uncover hidden opportunities to sell their personal service, and they know how to recognize growing and shrinking markets. They know how to customize their service according to their customer's needs and know how to outlast and outshine their competitors. Great salespeople are also able to negotiate the price of their personal service to maximize their profit/compensation.

This book will show you how to move from being simply a job seeker to a superstar seller of your personal service. You will learn how to make yourself the ideal candidate in the eyes of the employer and also how to get the best salary for your work.

If you have never thought of yourself as a salesperson, I want you to know that you have been one all your life. Your entire life is a continuous process of communicating, persuading and influencing other people on your ideas. Your ability to sell your personal service to others will determine the level of success you achieve in your career and life.

Many people think a salesperson is someone who convinces other people to do something they don't want to do. Or, they think salespeople take advantage of others. This book, however, will show you how to do the opposite. You will learn how to show and give value to employers in a way that will make them want to hire you.

Being a salesperson of your personal service is simply the act of giving: giving time, attention, counsel, education, empathy and value. The word "sell" actually comes from the Old English word "sellan," which means "to give."

After transitioning from a sales professional to a career coach, I realized that I really moved from selling products and services to teaching others how to better sell and market themselves to employers.

Introduction

This gives me the unique perspective about the interview process I share with you.

There are over 3,000 books about interviewing; however, mine is different because it's short, simple, to the point and applies the principle of successful salespeople to the job search process.

It is organized in a way that breaks down each part of the interview process, from the initial interview to salary negotiation. It is my absolute pleasure to share this information with you.

Chapter 1

The Job Seeker's Winning Philosophy

The Winning Edge Theory says that the difference between top performers and average performers is always very small. Top performers just do certain things a certain way a little better each day.

For a job seeker, this means there is only a slight difference between the exceptional one who lands the job and the average one who gets the rejection letter in the mail. The difference is in the job seeker's philosophy.

Success as a job seeker is an inner game. The philosophy of the person searching for a job is what will make the difference in his or her success. There is a direct relationship between a job seeker's philosophy and their success in selling their personal service to their ideal employer. This philosophy is the one of always giving value.

Yes, having a great resume, awesome interviewing ability, a strong professional network etc. contribute to having success in a job interview. However, a person's philosophy dictates the approach and direction one takes to the job search process.

A value-giving philosophy turns into a value-driven attitude, which leads to value-giving actions that cause positive results that lead to a positive lifestyle and career.

This philosophy causes one to approach prospective employers with a "What can I do for you?" attitude. On the other hand, a value-taking/entitlement philosophy makes one approach employers with a "Do you have a job for me?" attitude, which is hardly ever effective. A value-giving philosophy says, "I'll demonstrate excellence so you can hire me," while a value-taking/entitlement philosophy says, "Hire me first, and then I'll demonstrate excellence."

There are two major obstacles to landing a new job:

1. Employers are afraid of making a mistake by hiring the wrong person
2.The job seeker's fear of rejection.

When you have a value-giving philosophy, you build up enough value for employers and gain the confidence necessary to trump any fear of rejection.

The value the employer perceives in you will also cancel his or her fear in hiring the wrong person for his or her company.

In a job I once had selling print and online advertising to local business owners, my initial approach was to think about the potential problems the business faced and the solutions I had to solve them. One of my customers was the owner of a furniture store. Before I approached her about advertising, I knew her business was in a part of town that didn't provide the company with high visibility to potential customers. I also found out through research that they weren't advertising with any suitable outlets I knew of around town. What I observed was that the low visibility yielded significantly less potential customers walking into her store than other furniture stores around town. And it was from my observations that I was able to see the value my advertising service could provide to her business. My value-giving perspective gave me the confidence to talk to her about my company, and it also allowed me to present solutions that eventually caused her to work with me in boosting her walk-in traffic through advertising.

Your mindset, throughout your entire interview, should be how you can show that you have more value to give than you take in compensation.

Chapter 2

Why Employers Hire Candidates

It's important to understand that employers hire for their own reasons, not ours. This may sound like common knowledge, but the biggest mistake of any job seeker is to try to get an employer to hire him or her because of his or her own personal reasons. Every time an employer hires someone new, it is an attempt to be better off as a result of doing so. They have three decisions to make when a position is open. They can hire you, someone else or no one.

Each job interview is an opportunity to analyze what need you will meet by filling the open position. You cannot begin to convince an employer of the value your personal service will provide until you understand what need you can satisfy. Once this is understood, you can structure your message to the employer to show how you will be able to satisfy that need.

According to Abraham Maslow, in his hierarchy of needs, some of the basic necessities of any individual are to be respected, admired and liked. Employers want you to have all the necessary qualifications in case they have to answer to someone else about their decision in hiring you. They want to make sure they will maintain the same or an increased level of respect and admiration as a result of bringing you on board. They also want to know that you will help them solve their current problems so they can look successful among their peers.

One of the basic rules of selling your personal service is to remember that employers don't buy features. They buy benefits, which means they will not hire you just because you have a certain kind of education; they will not hire you simply because you've held certain positions in the past. They will hire you because you can benefit their business in some way. For example, if you are talking to a sales manager, he or she may be concerned with how you have increased sales in the past to determine how you might do so with the company in the future. If you are talking to an operations manager, he or she may be focused on cutting costs and making things more efficient. This person would want to know how you have done this in the past to learn how you might do this for them in the future.

Why Employers Hire Candidates

Your job as a job seeker is to find out the key benefits a prospective employer is searching for in a new hire. Also, your job is to ask questions skillfully and listen carefully. If you ask the right questions during an interview and listen long enough, the employer will reveal the key benefit he or she wants by hiring you. If you are being interviewed by a group of people, keep in mind there is always a general benefit they are all looking for in a candidate. In later chapters, you will learn which questions are the right ones and discover that sometimes, you can determine the potential key benefit from the job description.

Many times, an employer's decision may be purely emotional. You could have all the necessary qualifications for the job and display how the employer will benefit from hiring you, but they just may not employ you because of emotional reasons. He or she simply may not like you or how you presented yourself. In an employer's mind, the caliber of how professional, well-dressed and groomed you are is a direct reflection of the quality of your personal service. The level of rapport the employer has developed with you is also an indication on how well they will be able to work with you. Later, you will learn how to properly present yourself through your wardrobe and develop instant rapport with the employer.

Often, before walking into a business owner's establishment to propose the idea of using my personal service of advertising his business online or in my newspaper, I would always make sure of a couple of things. I had to be sure I was properly dressed to convey my professionalism and that I was ready to conduct business. I also had to make sure I understood the value I was presenting to the business owner. I knew he would not invest in advertising space in my newspaper or on my website simply because they were very well-known. The value for him was in how many qualified customers the advertisements could bring his business and boost his sales. To learn more about key benefits, I had to talk with him long enough, while skillfully listening and asking questions in a way that revealed how he wanted his business to be marketed to the public. Once I understood this, I was able to show him how he could achieve his marketing goals through my newspaper and website. Using this technique, the business owner hired my newspaper company and I to market his business online and in print multiple times. The same way I was able to do this is the same way you can convey your value to employers.

As long as you are focusing all your attention on the needs and wants of the employer, you will be marketing your personal service effectively in a professional way.

Chapter 3

Creatively Selling Yourself to Employers

Creatively selling yourself and personal service to employers begins with not only having a strong understanding of the business your potential employer is in, but also knowing how your personal service can help them achieve their goals. When preparing for a job interview, you need to be ready to present yourself in the best possible way to an employer in two steps. The first is to learn about the company, and the second is to explore how your personal service can provide the key benefit the employer is looking for in a new hire.

Step 1

Your research needs to answer the following questions:

What is the full name of the company?
What industry does this company operate in?
What are the products and services it provides?
What is the history of the company?
What are the organizational mission and goals of this company?
How is the company doing financially?
What is the organizational structure (divisions, subsidiaries, etc.)?
Where is the company located (main and branch locations)?

These questions can be answered simply by using the following resources:

Published Materials: This can consist of newspapers, journals or blogs. Try doing an online search of "[the company name] + news" to find any up-to-date information written about the company. You may do this search using google.com, yahoo.com or bing.com.

Annual Report: The company's annual report can serve as a source of information on how the company is doing financially. The report can also serve as a source of questions during the actual interview.

The Company Website: During an interview, it will already be assumed that you have browsed the company's website in its entirety. This means that it is important for you to familiarize yourself with the information found there.

Company Employees: People who are currently or were previously employed at the company you are interviewing with can serve as a great source for insider information you would not normally be privy to as an outsider. You can gain access to these people by requesting informational interviews of those who would be a peer on LinkedIn. By doing a search of the company on the site, you can find numerous employees who currently work for the company and have a profile there. A simple letter through LinkedIn, stating the following, will help to land you an informational interview with a current or former employee of the company:

Dear Mr./Ms./Mrs._____,

["Name of someone" suggested I contact you because you could give me the information I need.] – (This sentence is optional; include if it applies to you).

I am looking to explore opportunities within your organization.

My objective is to transition my career to "industry type or job function."

I would very much appreciate the opportunity to meet with you or talk over the phone for half an hour to introduce myself, discuss your work environment and gain advice on how someone with my background and experience can best position myself to work for your organization.
Would it be possible for us to set up a mutually convenient time to meet or speak over the phone?

Best Regards,

Obi Okere

In Chapter 7, you will learn how to conduct an informational interview once someone grants it to you.

Step 2

This step is broken into three parts. Part A will have you tally all of your major life accomplishments. In Part B, you will analyze those accomplishments. And Part C will have you apply those accomplishments to what the employer will want to know to make a hiring decision about you.

Part A

Creatively Selling Yourself to Employers

Tally 21 of the biggest personal accomplishments you have had within your whole career, whether you were paid or acted as a volunteer. They serve as examples of when you performed well in the past. Employers will not hire you only for the potential your skills can bring to their business. They also want to see how you have demonstrated excellence in the past to determine how you might exhibit excellence for them in the future. As you are listing your accomplishments, make sure that these are achievements you enjoyed achieving.

1. _____
2. _____
3. _____
4. _____
5. _____
6. _____
7. _____
8. _____
9. _____
10. _____
11. _____
12. _____
13. _____
14. _____
15. _____
16. _____
17. _____
18. _____
19. _____

20. _____
21. _____

Part B

In this part, you will choose your top 10 accomplishments and analyze them using the SOAR technique. SOAR is an acronym for Situation, Obstacles, Actions and Results. This part alone will properly prepare your answers to any questions and stories about your previous performance an interviewer might ask you to see how you performed in the past. You may also combine both the actions and results of each accomplishment to create strong bullet points for each of the job positions on your resume.

EX.

Situation - Describe the situation.	Obstacles - Describe the obstacles you faced.	Actions - List the actions you took.	Results - Describe the results you helped obtain.
1. Completed analysis to determine the cost to bring a new technology into the mobile phone	Creating a technical baseline with Engineers, collecting appropriate/useable data and methods to extrapolate to other platforms.	Developed a close relationship with engineers, worked with senior analysts to create a plan for data collection, minimized rework by meeting with the analyst before	Estimate was used in the final analysis report. Received a promotion as a result.

Creatively Selling Yourself to Employers 17

| market. | | me and utilized our leadership to open doors. | |

Situation - Describe the situation	Obstacles - Describe the obstacles you faced	Actions - List the actions you took	Results - describe the results you helped obtain
1.			
2.			
3.			
4.			
5.			
6.			
7.			
8.			
9.			
10.			

Part C

In this section, you will compare the needs and wants of the employer based on what you have noticed in the job description and what you know about yourself. Use data from Part B to determine where your major accomplishments match the employer's needs. Complete the chart below.

Job requirements/Potential needs of the employer	Credentials and past accomplishments that show you can serve the employer's needs
1.	
2.	
3.	
4.	
5.	
6.	

Part C will serve as your reference for the major reasons you are the ideal candidate for the job you are interviewing for.

Chapter 4

Tools to Bring With You to the Interview

A job interview is simply a sales meeting. It is your opportunity to consult with the employer, learn about the company's current challenges and present your personal service as a solution and a source for the key benefit they are looking for. However, even if your personal service is the "right" solution for the employer, it will not be seen as such if it is not presented properly. It is much like the difference between receiving a wrapped and an unwrapped gift for Christmas or your birthday. A wrapped gift allows the giver to present their gift in a better manner than with an unwrapped gift.

There are four keys tools to use during a job interview that will make or break how your personal service is presented. These tools are:
- Your Resume
- A Notepad
- 3x5 index cards
- Your clothes

The rest of this chapter will explain how you can maximize the use of each tool.

Your Resume

Be sure to bring at least five copies of your resume with you so you always have one for yourself and the interviewer(s). It can serve as a great reference and memory jogger when talking about your experience and accomplishments.

A Notepad

A notepad is necessary to jot down some of the key benefits the interviewer is looking for in an ideal candidate and the reasons why they might not hire you. You can also take notes of some of the challenges they are experiencing in their company and the possible solutions you might be able to provide. After the interview, this information will

Tools to Bring With You to the Interview 21

be important to use in your follow-up letter as you share reasons why they should either hire or call you back for the next stage of the interview process.

3x5 Index Cards

These cards are critical in helping you present yourself in the best way possible to the interviewer. It's okay to bring these cards into the interview and reference them from time to time. On these cards, you will have the following information:
- Bullet points on how you will artfully give a brief background of yourself when asked.
- Answers to the questions you fear they will ask you.
- Key points about yourself you want to stress during the interview.
- Questions you may have for the interviewer.

Your Clothes

What you wear to your job interview can make a big impact on your presentation to the interviewer. Your outfit gives them clues as to whether or not you understand and can fit within their corporate culture. Whether you are a recent school graduate or already have years of working experience, you can benefit from this section. Fortunately, you don't have to spend your life savings in order to properly present yourself.

General Rules

Do your homework
- Wait discretely outside your potential employer's office during lunch, and observe how everyone is dressed as they are walking outside (don't do this on casual Friday and get the wrong impression).
- Ask anyone you know who works there what the usual dress code is.

Dress two positions higher than the position you are applying for.
- You can always gain credit if you're overdressed, but you will lose credit if you're underdressed.

Rules for Men

Wear a Suit
- Navy, gray and black, in a solid or pinstripe, are great suit colors that are dark neutrals and allow an interviewer to picture you in a future management position. Avoid plaids and other bold patterns.
- Make sure the suit jacket has no more than two or three buttons and fits properly.

Jackets with more than three buttons are very trendy.
- For jackets with two buttons, button the top one only. For jackets with three, button the top and middle only.
- Wearing plain front or pleated slacks that are properly tailored will give you a very neat look. Make sure your pants are the right length and waist size for your body to avoid a sloppy look. When in doubt, consult the personnel of a men's suit store; they are trained to know the proper fit of men's suits.

Dress Shirt
- White, ivory and light blue shirts are classic choices.
- Avoid dark colors such as black, charcoal, navy blue, purple and burgundy.
- Avoid bright colors such as pink, apple green and yellow.
- You may choose between two collar types: a point collar or a spread collar. A button down collar is not appropriate to wear to an interview with or without a tie.
- Avoid cuff links. They can be seen as too flashy.
- Wear barrel cuff shirts with one button at the cuff.
- Show a quarter inch of your dress shirt at the bottom of your jacket sleeve.

Shoes, Belt and Tie
- The bottom of your tie should land right at your belt.
- Classic choices for tie colors are burgundy, gold and red.
- Avoid ties that are very flashy with bright colors.
- Striped ties also work very well.
- Oxfords, wing tipped, cap-toe, dress boots and monk strap shoes are appropriate men's styles to wear to an interview.
- Make sure your dress shoes are properly shined.
- Your belt color should match your shoe color.
- You shoe color should either be black, navy blue or brown.

Overall Appearance
- Be sure that you are neatly shaved.
- Your hair should be neatly styled.
- Avoid perfumes and colognes. Your interviewer might be allergic to the smell.
- Be sure to keep your fingernails neatly trimmed and clean.
- Avoid wearing any more jewelry than a conservative watch and one ring.

Rules for Women

Your Suit

- Suits in the colors of black, gray, navy blue, tan, brown, deep green, burgundy and plum are always good choices.
- Avoid any suit with a busy pattern, which will distract from your face and your overall professional image.
- Either a skirt or pants are acceptable. However, with organizations that are very conservative, a skirt will be more acceptable.
- Skirts should fall at the knee or just below.
- Pants should have a tailored fit without being too tight.

Blouse and Shirt
- Wear a blouse or collared shirt with a high or crew neck.
- White, ivory and light blue are the best color choices.
- Wear cotton or silk fabrics, and avoid sheer blouses.
- Modest V and scoop neck are also acceptable as long as your cleavage isn't revealed.

Shoes
- Wear basic, conservative pumps in a neutral color that complements your suit.
- Avoid heels higher than 2.5 inches.

Underwear
- A bra is a must. Be sure not to let it show through your shirt or blouse.
- Panty hose are also a must with your skirt.

- Carry a spare pair in case you get a run.

Accessories
- Use a briefcase instead of a purse.
- Pearl or diamond studs or small gold hoops are appropriate.
- Limit your rings to one on each hand.
- Avoid large bracelets.
- Wearing a leather watch is appropriate.
- When it comes to jewelry, less is more.

Hair
- Your hair should be simply styled.
- Avoid hairstyles that hide your face.
- A ponytail or a simple bun is appropriate.

Makeup and Perfume
- Your makeup should be conservative and not noticeable.
- Avoid perfume because your interviewer might be allergic.

Chapter 5

The Interview Process

Your job interview/sales meeting will begin a process that will have one of three outcomes: You will either get hired for the job, receive a message saying they have hired someone else or get no message at all. This process cannot be left to chance. Therefore, you must plan in advance how you will use the whole meeting to show how you not only are a better choice than the other candidates, but that you have much more to offer than you can take in payment. You must also demonstrate that you have more value to give than other candidates who are also in the running for the position. By following the steps outlined in this chapter, you will be prepared to articulate your value during an interview in such a way that creates an irresistible opportunity for you to get hired.

The interview process is broken into five stages:
- The Introduction
- Information Giving
- Information Gathering
- The Closing
- Follow-up

The rest of this chapter is devoted to walking you through each stage.

The Introduction

Usually, at the beginning of a job interview, the first question is always some form of "Can you tell me a little about yourself?" When asking this question, employers don't want you to list all of your life and career events since birth. They are really asking you to tell them why you are the right candidate for them to hire. This is your opportunity to set the tone for the rest of the interview by telling your story. Conveying your story allows you to talk about yourself in a compelling way that answers the following three questions:

1. What have you done before?
2. Why do you want this position and why now?
3. Why should we hire you?

Although these questions seem simple to answer,

many people get stuck or fumble on the last one. I've come across many professionals who seem to think that saying you are hardworking, a team player, a driven professional, etc. is sufficient enough to answer this question thoroughly. Most of those descriptors, however, are subjective and don't allow an employer to measure your performance. Employers want to hear what you have accomplished in the past so they can determine what you may be able to do for them in the future. You're not hired based on your potential; you are hired based on your demonstrated excellence. You can use your top three relevant accomplishments from chapter three to construct your story.

Your story should have the following structure:
1. The "Beginning" – This is where you went to school or started your career.
2. Your Interest – This is what inspired you to pursue your current career.
3. Your Accomplishments – These are relevant past achievements the employer wants to hear.
4. Why You're Here Today – Your answer will depend on how you complete the following sentence:
    - "I'm interviewing here today because....."
5. Your Future – This is where you share your long-term goals and how working at this company helps you move closer to them.

If telling your story takes more than two minutes, you may find that the interviewer has stopped paying attention to what you're saying. Try to keep it concise and to the point. Develop your story in advance, practice it on friends and family, and look for ways to make it brief and concise while still fully articulating your value.

Here is an example of my introduction, which I once shared during an interview when I was asked to tell about myself:

My name is Obi Okere. I received an Electrical Engineering degree from Rutgers University. In the Fall, I will start a master's degree program in Adult Learning and Leadership at Columbia University. After college, I got my start in sales, where I have worked in the advertising, publishing and insurance industries. While working at XYZ Company, I developed an interest in sales and corporate training. As a result of my interest, I started to seek out various volunteer opportunities to deliver talks, presentations and trainings with different groups and organizations on different professional development topics. My biggest three accomplishments include:

- Helping to increase the sales of sales associates at XYZ Company by 15 percent through the sales trainings I delivered.
- Receiving 5/5 satisfaction ratings for delivering career management trainings to students and professionals at the National Urban League Young Professionals Group and at Rutgers University.
- Coaching over 50 clients, one-on-one, over the course of one year to perform self-assessments and develop job search marketing plans.

Through my experience, I have honed my skills in performance consulting, coaching, training and public speaking. I am interested in being a training project manager because it allows me to apply my passion and skills in designing and delivering training presentations that help other people perform better at their jobs. In the future, I see myself growing my career in learning and development. I see this company as the best place to do so.

Information Giving

For many job seekers, the toughest part of preparing for an interview is being ready to answer any question asked. In a competitive job market, employers are not only trying to figure out if you're the best candidate, they are also looking to ask tough questions to disqualify you from the selection process and make their job easier. The most important mindset to have when answering these questions is one where you see it is a game. The interview process is a game to determine who can present him or herself in the best way to the employer. Seeing this process as a game allows you to expand your creativity as you consider how you will play each questioned asked. Generally, there are really only five major questions you will be asked during the interview. They are:

1. **Why do you want to work for our company?**
When answering this question, you want to consider how working at this company will fit into

your long-term career goals. You also want to think about what you really like about the company.

2. **What would be the benefit of having you work at our company?**
If you've completed the exercises in chapter three, you will be able to answer this question by talking about what you have accomplished in the past and how you can achieve similar or even better results with their company.

3. **What kind person are you?**
Employers will ask four forms of this question. They simply want to know if you are easy to work with and can fit into the existing culture. The first form comes as a behavioral question, beginning with the phrase, "Tell me about a time when you...." You can reference your past accomplishments and use the SOAR method (explained in chapter three) to explain the situation, the obstacles you faced, the actions you proceeded with and the results you created to answer this question succinctly.

The second form of this question is asking you about your weaknesses. This question stems from the fear that you might have a major character flaw that would prevent you from performing well on the job. You can simply answer it by not only mentioning a real and correctable weakness, but also mentioning how you have dealt with the weakness in the past. You can also take a step further and demonstrate how your weakness is actually a strength that would allow you to perform differently than other candidates.

The third form of this question can come in a couple of different ways: Why did you leave your last job? Or what was the relationship of you and your former boss? Whether you were fired, downsized or quit, you must always speak positively about your previous boss or company, and spin your separation as an opportunity you proactively sought as you were looking to build your long-term career.

Finally, the fourth form can come in the style of why you have gaps in your resume. Answer this question by talking about some of your volunteer or consulting work, your work study in school to gain some new skills or your work simply trying to find your mission/career direction in life.

4. **What makes you different from the other candidates we are interviewing for the same position?**

While answering this question, consider the unique approach you have taken to achieve many of your accomplishments to date. Your unique method is what makes you different from other candidates. Also, from the research you did in chapter three, think about how your unique approach and industry knowledge will help the employer solve their problem in a way better than anyone else can.

5. **Can I afford to pay you?**

At some point during the interview, the employer may ask for your salary requirements. The game in this question is that if your requirements are too high, they will not want to consider you. On the other hand, if your requirements are too low, you might be leaving money on the table during the negotiation. The employer's perceived value of you may also decrease because you are asking for much less in payment than they expected to give. The way you go about answering this question will be thoroughly covered in chapter six.

Information Getting

Toward the latter part of the interview, the interviewer will ask if you have any questions for him. At this point, great questions are critical to your interview's success. There are plenty of reasons to ask good questions during this time. The following are the most important:

- It helps you understand the employer's current challenges and problems they will need a new candidate to solve.
- Good questions help establish good rapport that will help create a comfort level where the interviewer will more freely reveal key information that allows you to customize how you will use your personal service for their unique situation.
- It helps you show how your qualifications are significantly different than the other candidates.
- Good questions can heighten your credibility with the employer, stimulate their thinking

and create a positive attitude about you and
the personal service you provide.

You shouldn't just ask any question for the sake of asking questions. You want to choose them carefully. The criteria you use to choose your questions will be based on what is important to you in a new job and the information you feel is missing in your understanding of the employer's needs and the responsibilities of the position.

The process of asking questions begins with identifying areas where you currently lack information about the job position. Take 15 minutes before the interview to ask yourself the following to help you determine the questions you will ask the employer:

Step 1: What do I need to know concerning what the employer is looking for in an ideal candidate?
Anyone with whom you interview can have a positive or negative impact on whether you either get hired or called for the next stage of the interview process. Each interviewer will also have a different perspective on what an ideal candidate would be. Because the roles played by your interviewers can be diverse, look at whether you know the names of and understand the background of everyone you are interviewing with. If you don't know, you can simply call or email the person who scheduled the interview and ask for the names of those people. They usually will not mind telling you this. Once you know their full names, you can look up their

profiles on LinkedIn or do a Google search of their names in quotes. Using the quotes allows you to search for the first and last name as a whole.

Consider putting yourself in their shoes, and think about each interviewer's expertise as it relates to the job you are interviewing for. For example, if you are interviewing for a marketing position with a person in the sales department, this person would have a perspective on how they want marketing to support the sales of the company.

Step 2: What do I need to know about the actual role and its responsibilities?
Consider how well you understand the requirements of the job position. Do you have enough information about the role to be able to directly relate it to your past accomplishments? How can you achieve the same, if not more, at their company?

Step 3: What do I need to know about the problems or challenges that the person hired will have to handle?
Think about whether you fully understand the kinds of problems the person hired would have to take care of all the time. Think about why these particular issues are important to the employer.

Step 4: What do I need to know about the company itself and the working environment?
Consider whether the culture of the company will

The Interview Process

fit in with your personality. Do you know if the existing environment is one where you can succeed?

After you go through the four previous steps, write down the information that is most important for you to know. You can then consider how you will phrase your question to get that information during the interview without getting very vague and unclear answers. Below, you will find a few questions you can use. You usually want to have three to five questions ready for each person you will interview with.

- What do you see ahead for your company in the next five years?

- What do you consider to be your firm's most important assets?

- What can you tell me about your new product or plans for growth?

- What happened to the last person who held this job?

- What were the major strengths and weaknesses of the last person who held this job?

- What types of skills do you NOT already have on board that you're looking to fill with a new hire?

- What is the overall structure of the company, and how does your department fit the structure?

- What are the career paths in this department?

- What would you consider to be the most important aspects of this job?

- What are the skills and attributes you value most for someone being hired for this position?

- Could you describe a typical day or week in this position?

- What are the most immediate challenges of the position that need to be addressed in the first three months?

- What are the performance expectations of this position over the first 12 months?

Closing

Many people will have a great interview but fail to close it properly. This is like offering a Christmas present without wrapping it. After asking all your questions, it is important to follow these five key steps to solidify your chances of getting the job:

1. Thank them for their time.

2. State how you feel about the job and why you feel that way ("I'm interested in the job because..."). Use this opportunity to also state three reasons why you would be a good fit for this position.

3. Ask: "Do you see me as a fit for this position?" Be very sincere and direct as you ask this question.

4. If they say NO, ask: "What are your major concerns about my qualifications?" Make sure you listen without interrupting the interviewer. Gather all of his or her objections about why you may not be a fit for the position. Answer each objection with a reason why it should not be a concern for the interviewer. Make sure you finish this step by asking: "Have I answered all of your concerns about offering me this position?" If the answer is NO, ask what their remaining concerns are and continue to address his or her objections.

If the answer is YES, ask: "Where do we proceed from here?" Or, "What is the next step?"

5. At this point, many people fail to ask for the job. Many assume that since they are there for the interview, it is already known they want the job. However, most companies will expect you to ask for

the job during the interview. You may say something to the effect of the following:

"After everything we discussed, I would like to be considered for this role. Where do we go from here?"

Or

"This opportunity matches my career goals, and I know I can do a really great job for you. Who are the other decision makers selecting who gets hired for this role?"

Make sure you say this with a lot of conviction and enthusiasm. Enthusiasm sells.

The Follow-up

After the interview, you want to send a follow-up letter either the night of or the day after it. The sooner you do it, the better. Typically, many job seekers use this letter to only say thank you for the opportunity to interview with a company. However, the mindset of a salesperson requires you to do more to influence the possibility of you getting called for the next stage of the interview process. This type of follow-up letter is better used as a tool in influencing the company's decision to call you back for another interview. It's also an opportunity to further address and defend any reasons why the company might not want to hire you. When constructing this letter, you want to ask yourself four questions:

1. When compared to my competitors, what might be their top two reasons for not wanting to hire me?
2. What are some of the major concerns the interviewer had about my candidacy for the job during the interview?
3. What are the three key reasons the employer should hire me?
4. What are some solutions I have to help solve some of the challenges the interviewer is dealing with in their department?

Your follow-up letter should have the following structure:

Four or Five Paragraphs
- The Opening:
  - Thank them for interviewing you.
- Summary of yourself and why they should hire you:
  - Two or three sentences.
- One or two paragraphs addressing their concern(s) for hiring you or sharing problem-solving ideas you have for their department

- Closing: What you'd like them to do:
  - Request to talk with them further about your ideas if you shared them.
  - Make it clear that you want the job:

- The interviewer will not simply assume this;
- This can be done by saying, "I would like to be considered for the next stage of the interview process," or "I would like to be considered for this job."

Chapter 6

The Psychology of Negotiation

So you have aced your job interview and got a job offer. It may or may not be the salary you expected. Your ability to leverage your negotiating power will depend on how well you best communicate your qualifications, value, benefits and performance to the employer in exchange for status, position, money and extra perks. You have the opportunity to increase your salary for the year by up to $10K or more and gain extra perks within five minutes. As you approach your salary negotiation strategy, consider how you can make compensation increase requests while still communicating you are giving more value than what you are being paid. You can effectively negotiate your salary by using the three step A.C.T. method:

- Analyze

- Collaborate
- Take it or leave it.

Situation:

The hiring manager calls you and offers you a job at $xx,xxx yearly base salary plus benefits. The goal here is to create a win-win situation between you and the employer. You may not get all you want, but what matters is that you are prepared through your research and that you do everything you can within the negotiation process. No matter what you are offered, your first response should be:

"Thank you for the offer. I'm very excited about the position and working at your company. Can I have a day to get back to you about this offer?"

At this point, you will now have bought yourself time to complete a three step A.C.T method so that you can know the best way to A.C.T. in the salary negotiating game. Through this method, you will be able to effectively plan your negotiating strategy for the following four common types of salary offers:
- Higher than the range you researched
- Low but not lower than the lowest figure you would accept
- Too low and below the lowest figure you would accept
- Your target salary

Analyze

It's important to analyze the financial value employers typically have for your personal service. If you are given an offer much lower than the pay rate you expected, you can find out if you should and can be paid more for your service. In order to conduct your research, use the Internet and other people within your network that may be familiar with the average pay for the position you are interviewing for. Online, you can visit payscale.com, glassdoor.com and salary.com for salary information. While doing your informational interviews – which you learned how to ask for in chapter three and how to conduct in chapter seven – you can ask questions about the starting salary of someone with your experience, skills and other qualifications for your prospective position. With this information, you will want to determine three things:
- Your target salary
- The lowest figure you would accept
- The salary range for which you will use to negotiate

Not only should you know your worth to an employer, you should also evaluate how you can show the employer you are worth a pay increase. Make a list of all the problems your prospective employer needs to solve (you learned how to do this in chapter five). Make another list of your top five key qualifications, accomplishments and experiences that will enable you to be a problem-solver. This is the information you will use for leverage in your negotiating process.

After determining your salary requirements, it is also important to evaluate other aspects of the offer, such as the additional employment benefits you will be given. You do not want to try to negotiate the base salary and benefits at the same time. This may cause you to get less than what you should on both. It is best to start with the base salary negotiations. Once you agree on a base salary, you can then negotiate additional benefits.

Consider and make a list (in order of importance) of the types of employment benefits you will need. These could be things such as:
- Job title
- Vacation time
- Educational reimbursement
- Flextime:
    - Time spent working from home vs. time spent in the office
- Benefits
- Timing your first review
- Relocation expenses
- Memberships
    - Gym
    - Professional Association

Collaborate with the Employer

After you have done your research and determined

your salary and employment benefit needs, it is now time to get back in touch with the employer. Whether the offer is verbal or in writing, it is best to conduct the negotiations verbally (via phone or in person).

The following is how to continue your conversation with your prospective employer for each of the four salary offer situations:

Higher than the range you researched

"Thank you again for the generous offer. I'm very excited about the position and working at your company. I will accept the salary you are offering. I do, however, have one point about the employment benefits that I would like to discuss further with you."

This is where you discuss the types of benefits you would like. Be sure to start the benefit conversation with the things most important to you.

Low but not lower than the lowest figure you would accept

"Thank you for the offer. I'm very excited about the position and working for you. The salary is less than what I was thinking. I did some research and found that the typical salary range for this position is from x to y. I assume that the lower end of that range is for people with little to no experience. My experience (name three things about your experience they value) would put me at around the (name the middle or higher end) of the range. I was wondering how much you can move towards this amount."

Too Low and below the lowest figure you would accept

"Thank you for the offer. I'm very excited about the company and working for you. I want to make sure this offer is for the same position we discussed where I (talk about the duties of the position).....Pause (let them respond).... According to (name an outside source such as salary.com), the average salary for this position is from x to y. Your offer is below that range. I was wondering how much you can move into this range."

Your Target Salary

In a situation like this, you can accept the offer, or you can ask for more. If you are going to ask for more, you want to think of some solid reasons, based on your experience, for why you deserve more in salary. You may respond with the following:

"Thank you for the offer. I'm very excited about the company and working for you. According to some research that I did on (name an outside source), the salary you named was at the (low or middle) part of the average salary for a position like this. Based on all of the responsibilities we talked about where I (name your top three responsibilities), my experience in (name your area of expertise) allows me to start performing right away. Is there any way you can move the salary into the higher part of this range?"

For each of the last three common scenarios, the hiring manager could counteroffer and say he/she can go up to $x amount. This is where you pause, for at least one second, and make your own counteroffer. He/she will accept that figure, give you another one or say they can't go higher than the new figure. You can accept, negotiate further, including additional benefits, ask for more time, or give them the least you would accept.

At some point, you will have negotiated, counter offered and reached a point where you've gotten to their maximum financial offer. Depending on the company you are negotiating with, you may see there are very strict policies on increasing a proposed salary and health benefits. This doesn't mean they won't have a separate budget for additional perks, such reimbursement on continuing education or an extra week of paid vacations. These things can be negotiated to make up for the rigidity of the company's compensation policies.

Take It or Leave It

At this point of the negotiation process, you will

have finalized a certain salary and employment benefits. The next step is to tell the employer you need another day to consider the offer. This is where you will finally decide whether or not you want to accept or reject the job offer. If you decide to accept, you can simply email the hiring manager with a summary of all the negotiation terms of your employment and your indication that you will be taking the job. You can also follow up with a phone call, referencing the email. If you decide not to take the job, you can simply call the hiring manager, thanking him or her for the offer and letting him/her know you respectfully decline.

Chapter 7

Creating More Interviews With More Employers

One of the most effective and underused job search techniques is the informational interview. According to quintcareers.com, one out of every 200 resumes results in a job offer. One out of every 12 informational interviews results in one job offer.

An informational interview is simply a meeting with another person who has experience, expertise or influence in an area you want to gain more information about. For a job seeker, informational interviews are critical in getting insider information about a particular industry, job function or company. This meeting can serve different purposes for various job seekers.

Specifically, this interview can help you do the following:

- Learn how to properly brand yourself for a career change to a specific field.
- Focus your career goals.
- Gain information on what growing industries need your skills and talents.
- Learn from hiring managers about their current and future needs for their department.
- Discover careers and jobs you never knew existed.
- Learn about the realities of working in a particular occupation.
- Discover the earning potential of a job in your prospective career.
- Learn the names and contact information of other people you can meet to help you land the job you want.

Through informational interviews, you can effectively connect with any hiring manager you want. The six degrees of separation theory is common knowledge to many people. We are only six people away from anyone else on the planet. In 2007, Jure Leskovec and Eric Horvitz revisited this theory through a study. They examined the data of 30 billion instant message conversations of 240 million Microsoft Messenger users. They found the average path length of one user to any other user was 6.6.

For any job seeker or person looking to strengthen their professional network, the application of the six degrees of separation theory can yield remarkable results. By the very process of networking with other people, we can reach anyone in the world in six steps or less. The challenge I find that many professionals face is that they apply this theory the wrong way.

Many times, job seekers make a new networking contact through an event, an online interaction on sites such as LinkedIn or through a friend. They may have an initial conversation where he or she interacts with their new contact, but often, they fail to follow up with that contact again. The real results of networking don't happen during the first interaction. A networking contact needs to take time to get to know the person and build trust. It's only after trust is built that a contact will start referring trusted friends and contacts to the job seeker. It takes multiple interactions with this person to build a high level of trust, which is necessary for permission to explore the contact's professional network.

If we were to consistently follow up with 10 first degree contacts that each referred 10 other people who successively each referred 10 more people, we would instantly have access to 1,000 people in our networks. If those 10 people were important, first-degree contacts who worked in the industry you are targeting for your job search, exploring their second- and third-degree contacts would help expose you to job opportunities that aren't advertised.

Your aim should be to have anywhere from five to 10 meetings with other people per week to have a very successful job search.

The way to conduct successful information interviews lies in the following steps:

Step 1: Create a Goal
Determine what you want to accomplish in your career and the type of information and people you need to know in order to move your career forward. For example, you may need to know which companies are expanding and how they will undertake that expansion because you are looking to make a career change into a new field.

Step 2: Identify and make contacts
Search your personal network, college alumni association and LinkedIn for people who may be able to give you information you need or connect you to people who will help you move your career forward.

Step 3: Conduct Research
Before contacting that person, research him or her through as many online channels (Google, LinkedIn, etc.) as you can to find out all the ways they are connected to the information you seek and the other people you want to know.

Step 4: Send a short letter
This letter can briefly introduce yourself, your background, your career goals and the information you are requesting. Ask for about 30 minutes of the person's time and his or her availability for a meeting.

Step 5: Arrange a time and place to talk

It is much easier to arrange a date and time for meetings that take place via phone. In-person meetings, on the other hand, are a bit more challenging to schedule. When meeting with a hiring manager, it is better to have the meeting in person than over the phone. An in-person meeting can help create more rapport that can lead to a job interview or a referral to another person who makes hiring decisions.

Step 6: Prepare for the meeting

Prepare a list of questions on 3x5 index cards to bring to the informational interview. This list ensures you don't forget to ask any questions during the meeting. Also, make sure to develop a two minute summary of your story (you learned this in chapter five) of your background and what you want to do next in your career. This way, you will be prepared to talk about yourself when the person you are meeting with inquires.

Step 7: End the meeting properly

At the end of the meeting, ask if there is anyone else the person suggests you talk to (i.e., their second-degree contacts) or if they have any other insight about the information you are seeking.

Step 8: Send a thank you note

After the meeting, send a note thanking the person for his/her time and help.

Step 9: Schedule a date in your calendar to follow up with this person to update them on the progress you have made, and ask if they know anyone else you could talk to or if they have heard of any new job opportunities you would be interested in.

Step 10: Repeat steps three through nine with your newly acquired contacts.

Chapter 8

Staying Motivated Throughout the Process

Most people would agree that landing a new job is a job in itself. For job seekers, this job search can sometimes be a lonely emotional roller coaster. There are times when a seeker can feel very good about their search progress, while at other times, he or she can be at an emotional low.

During the process of a job search, it's important to stay motivated so you maintain the momentum of actively and creatively uncovering multiple opportunities. Maintaining one's motivation is not just about keeping a positive perspective. It is also about having a structure in place to get out of the emotional lows quickly when they happen.

Here are my top six ways to stay motivated during a job search:

Build your vision.
Take some time to envision your perfect job. With this vision in mind, write down all of its components. You may use magazine clippings to paint a collage as well. Refer to this vision daily to remind you of what you are working towards in your job search.

Celebrate your victories.
Usually, we know we are doing a good job if someone else says we are. Create small games with goals for yourself each day and week. They could be contacting a certain number of people in a day for an informational interview or attending a particular number of networking events in a week. Additionally, one could be the number of people you actually have an informational interview with each week. Track the daily and weekly results of your game, and reward yourself with things for achieving your goals.

Limit your exposure to the news.
The news can be very depressing, especially when there are constant reports on how bad, slow or tough the job market is.

Stay away from negative people.
They will only have bad things to say about your job search. Therefore, surround yourself with other

people who are already employed, keep a positive perspective and make you feel good about yourself.

Schedule time for fun.
Make sure to take a break at least once a week, and schedule something fun to do. This could be a hobby, time at the gym, sports, an event or time with your family and friends.

Hire a career coach.
A career coach can help you devise a reliable strategy that will make your job search more effective and measurable. He or she can also provide the support you need to stay motivated and confident throughout your job search.

About the Author

Obi Okere is a certified career coach who helps career professionals clarify their career path and land their dream job. To date Obi has coached and trained over 1000 people through one on one sessions, live workshops, and seminars. He has done career management presentations for organizations and institutions such as New York University, Deutsche Bank, the National Urban League, the National Black MBA Association, Rutgers University, and Fordham University.

Obi leverages his unique perspective as a former sales executive to show professionals how to better sell themselves and increase their work performance. He is also a Master's Degree candidate at Columbia University in Organizational Leadership and Adult Learning.

Visit www.realizeyourpeak.com

www.ingramcontent.com/pod-product-compliance
Lightning Source LLC
Chambersburg PA
CBHW061517180526
45171CB00001B/224